Leonardo DiCaprio

AN ILLUSTRATED STORY

CAROLINE WESTBROOK

HAMLYN

The author would like to thank the following for their assistance and support: Julian Brown, Leslie Bunder, Karen O'Grady, Pamela Melnikoff, Helen and David Westbrook, Ian and Marsha Westbrook, Hugh Westbrook and Melissa Green, UUNET UK, AOL UK, (http://www.carrera.co.uk). And last but by no means least, a special big thank you to Good Ghost (we still have imaginary friends!. . .)

Caroline Westbrook can be e-mailed at:
caroline@dial.pipex.com

Publishing Director Laura Bamford
Executive Editor Julian Brown
Editor Karen O'Grady
Design Richard Scott
Picture Research Maria Gibbs
Production Mark Walker

CONTENTS

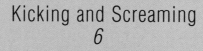

First published in Great Britain in 1997
by Hamlyn,
an imprint of Reed Consumer Books Limited
Michelin House, 81 Fulham Road,
London SW3 6RB
and Auckland, Melbourne, Singapore and Toronto

Copyright © 1997 Reed Consumer Books Limited

Reprinted 1998

ISBN 0 600 592731

A catalogue record for this book is available from the British Library

Printed by Butler and Tanner, Frome, Somerset.

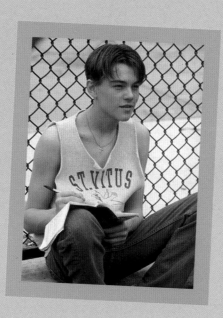

1

Kicking and Screaming

The clapperboard reads:

UNIVERSAL STUDIOS.
PRODUCER
DIRECTOR
SCENE   TAKE   ROLL

DATE   PROD. NO.

From the Hollywood slums to the sit-com world, Leonardo's upbringing was far from conventional

Leonardo DiCaprio was born to be a star. At the age of only 22, this blond Californian is seemingly loved by absolutely everybody, from a globe-wide body of fans, who cherish his boyish good looks and astounding acting talent, to the critics who just can't praise him enough. Not for nothing has DiCaprio been pronounced the best new actor of his generation. His performances in the likes of *What's Eating Gilbert Grape?* (For which he was Oscar-nominated), and the more recent *William Shakespeare's Romeo And Juliet* prove that he really is more than just a pretty face – he is a captivating screen presence. And yet somehow he still manages not to sell out – by choosing interesting roles over potential box office money spinners he has won himself an enormous degree of respect with everybody who sees his work.

In fact, there's something altogether different about Leonardo DiCaprio – while a lot of his peers appear introverted and prefer to shun the limelight, Leonardo takes it all in his stride, and despite playing a string of intense, tortured young men onscreen, is described as a lively hyperactive figure behind the camera, who spends most of his time joking around with his co-stars and is happiest living a comparatively normal existence away from the cameras. 'I think it has to do with me not investing everything in my job,' he said in a recent interview. 'All these actors think that the blood through their veins is fuelled by acting, but I'm happier hanging out with my friends when I'm not working.' If world domination is just a step away, he is clearly making no attempt to avoid it. Such an attitude probably stems from what can only be described as an unconventional childhood.

Leonardo Wilhelm DiCaprio was born on November 11, 1974 in Los Angeles, California, the only child of German mother Irmelin (none too surprisingly, Leonardo speaks fluent German) and Italian father George. He also has a stepbrother, Adam. His striking first name came about during a trip that his mother made to Italy's Uffizi Gallery while she was pregnant; while admiring a Leonardo Da Vinci painting, her unborn son decided to pitch in with a swift kick, something she interpreted as a message telling her what to name the child.

Although he was brought up just a stone's throw from Tinseltown, Leonardo's early life was far from glamorous. Living in what he later described as the slums of Hollywood, his hippy parents had split up before he had even blown out the candles on his first birthday cake, although they never divorced and remain close friends to this day, working together on managing their son's career (his mother concentrates on the financial side of things, while his dad surveys the dozens of scripts that come crashing through the letter box every week). Their son, likewise, is equally close to his parents, so much so that he only moved out of his mother's house last year.

However, Leonardo's upbringing was also a bohemian one that proved to be enormously

Above: *Parenthood:* **Gil (Ed Begley Jr. takes on nephew Jerry (Leonardo) in the annual backyard basketball championships**

Smash sit-com *Roseanne* provided Leonardo with one of his many TV appearances

Above: Leonardo joined forces with the world's most famous collie in *The New Lassie* – but only for two episodes

Opposite: Leonardo as he appeared in *Growing Pains*, playing homeless teen Luke Brower

influential on his later life: his dad ran a business from his garage, producing underground comic books and comic arts, while his mother quit her more conventional job as a legal secretary to manage Leonardo's acting career when it began to take off. Throughout Leonardo's childhood, the house would be full of high profile visitors, including writers such as Charles Bukowski and fellow underground satirical comic artist Robert Crumb.

From an early age, Leonardo was restless and hyperactive, especially in the classroom, and at both his schools, the Center For Enriched Studies and John Marshall High School, he got more of a kick out of being the class clown, and providing lunchtime entertainments in the playground for his friends, than battening down to his studies. He often cheated in lessons (especially maths) and skipped homework altogether. 'I was always known as the crazy little kid,' he says, 'and I never got the knack of school. I could never focus on things I didn't want to learn. Instead I used to take half the school and do breakdancing skits with my friends in front of them at lunchtime.'

But he had already found a way in which to channel his energies. Long before starting school, acting – of a sort – had beckoned, and when Leonardo was three, he made his debut on *Romper Room,* a long-running educational show for children beamed across the TV sets of America at an impossibly early hour. Even then, he seemed incapable of settling down, and before long he was unceremoniously removed from the set due to his unruly behaviour. It was his last appearance in front of a camera for nine years.

During this time, Leonardo was blazing the audition trail, with comparatively little success; and at the age of ten he nearly quit the business altogether after one agent suggested, none too tactfully, that he alter his 'wrong' haircut and change his name to the far less foreign sounding Lenny Williams. It was incidents such as these which left Leonardo disillusioned with the commercialism of the industry he was trying to break into. But with his parents encouragement, and the added incentive of his stepbrother's appearance on a hugely successful commercial for Golden Grahams cereal, he kept going, and finally landed himself an agent at the age of 14.

Leonardo's initial work was in television, appearing in over 30 commercials, and educational films with such titles as *Mickey's Safety Club* and *How To Deal With A Parent Who Takes Drugs*. When he was 15, he also had a part of the blink-and-you'll-miss-it variety in the TV series of *Parenthood*, the spin-off show from Ron Howard's hugely successful 1990 film, which starred Steve Martin as the neurotic head of an ever-expanding family, and also featured a very young looking Keanu Reeves as his niece's race car-fixated boyfriend. But it wasn't long before the TV series began to pour in, and he made guest appearances on a whole range of popular programmes, including the soap opera *Santa Barbara*, sitcom smash *Roseanne* and *The Outsiders*, a TV spin-off series from the 1983 hit film of the same name. Also on the agenda were two episodes of *The New Lassie*, But Leonardo did not have to share centre stage with a heroic collie dog for long. At the age of 16, he landed his first regular TV role, on the hit series *Growing Pains*.

The show, a long-running success in the States which strangely failed to make it across the pond, was a sitcom aimed at teens, and extremely popular due to its handsome star, Kirk Cameron, who played Seavers, a well-meaning teen coping with the tribulations of adolescence. Leonardo appeared on the scene in 1990 and stayed for two series (24 episodes), starring as a streetwise homeless kid whom Cameron's character took pity on and invited into his home. Although it did wonders for DiCaprio's career and thrust him into the public eye more than anything he had done previously, the experience is not one he looks back on fondly. 'I couldn't bear it,' he has since said 'everybody was bright and chipper. But I got to know what I didn't want to do.'

Whatever Leonardo's opinions may have been of the show, the one thing it did prove to the hordes of viewers who tuned in every week was that he showed a good deal more potential than his co-stars. And while Kirk Cameron disappeared into relative obscurity once *Growing Pains* finally wound down, the co-star who had inadvertently stolen the limelight from his leading man went on to focus his attention fully on his greatest ambition – getting into the movies.

Leonardo takes a well-earned break from starring in sit-coms

Leonardo makes his debut with Kirk Cameron (right) on *Growing Pains* as Luke, the homeless teen accused of pilfering Jason's (Alan Thickie, left) wine collection

Not that Leonardo hadn't already shown his face in the multiplexes. In 1991, while still on the show, he took on his first starring role in a movie – that of Josh in cheapie horror sequel *Critters 3*. The latest in a franchise that had been marginally successful in the 1980's thanks to its release soon after the smash hit *Gremlins*, the series concentrates on a group of alien furballs invading earth and causing all manner of havoc – in this case, imprisoning the residents of a tower block in a plot not entirely dissimilar to disaster classic *The Towering Inferno*.

It's not the first time that a household name has turned to low-budget horror to make their mark on the movies – Brad Pitt's debut was in the equally forgettable slasher spoof *Cutting Class,* while *Friends'* star Jennifer Aniston was the love interest of a decidedly anti-social green monster in *Leprechaun* – but nonetheless, for obvious reasons, *Critters 3* does not figure too highly on the DiCaprio CV.

A much better choice for Leonardo turned out to be a small role in the teen psycho-thriller *Poison Ivy,* a film notable for marking the comeback of actress Drew Barrymore. As fellow student Guy, DiCaprio provided moral support to *Roseanne* star Sara Gilbert, who stars as Sylvie, an awkward loner befriending the beautiful new girl in class (Barrymore), only to discover that her new best pal has a major crush on her father and will stop at nothing (including murder) to get what she wants.

Poison Ivy was an enjoyable, tense thriller which didn't exactly register with cinema audiences but has since made its mark on video, although admittedly Leonardo was somewhat overshadowed by the superb performances from the two female leads.

But with his film career beginning to take off nicely, it would only be a matter of time before he did leave an impression of his own, and he did it by starring with none other than Robert De Niro.

2

This Boy's Break

Leonardo's move into movies grabs a wealth of attention

This Boy's Life gave Leonardo his big break in movies

This Boy's Life: Leonardo as Toby, attempts to bond with stepfather Dwight (Robert De Niro)

Few actors can boast that they have appeared on screen alongside Robert de Niro before they reach their 18th birthday, while even fewer could be said to have out-acted the man himself. However, Leonardo DiCaprio not only has the former credit on his ever-expanding list of roles, but was regarded by many to have achieved the latter at the same time – giving him the 'big break' he had been waiting for since the age of five. It's all thanks to a little-known movie called *This Boy's Life,* which may have made a swift exit from cinemas but had more impact on Leonardo's career than he could ever have dreamed of.

Set in the 1950's, and based on a true story by writer Tobias Wolff, *This Boy's Life* is a grim, but compelling coming-of-age tale directed by British filmmaker Michael Caton-Jones (who also shouted the orders on World War II drama *Memphis Belle* and Scottish epic *Rob Roy*). Ellen Barkin (*Sea Of Love*, *The Fan*) is Caroline Wolff, single parent to three boys, including eldest son Toby (DiCaprio), living in smalltown America, and being taunted by an abusive boyfriend.

In order to escape the regular beatings, Barkin and son flee to begin a new life in the dour, grey town of Concrete, Washington, where she meets and rapidly marries a local mechanic, Dwight (De Niro), not stopping to think of the possible consequences.

He, however, turns out to be an alcoholic every bit as abusive as the man they have escaped, taking an instant dislike to his new stepson in the process, and when the domestic violence begins again Toby takes the brunt of his new parent's abuse: Dwight steals the money from his paper round and refuses to buy him basketball shoes so that he is forced to play barefoot.

None too surprisingly, Toby begins hanging around with the wrong crowd and getting a reputation in the neighbourhood for being troublesome, although in-between there's also time for a spot of teen romance and a touching relationship with his openly gay best friend. (Jonah Blechman). When his mother proves to be resigned to her husband's tendencies, it is down to Toby to convince her to flee Concrete and set up home elsewhere. Only then can mother and sons renew their bonds.

This particular role proved an extraordinary challenge from the start, with Leonardo beating 400 other young actors to land the part of Tobias Wolff, and quitting his regular role on *Growing Pains* to make the movie. Then there was the task of working with Robert De Niro, often lauded as the finest actor of his generation. A daunting prospect certainly – initially an actor as renowned as De Niro would seem unapproachable – but despite their onscreen hatred for one another, the pair hit it off tremendously once the cameras were switched off, DiCaprio's reputation for being laid-back and easy-going on sets coming to the fore. DiCaprio has since said

that he cherished the whole experience, crediting De Niro for his support and encouragement, and for providing him with vital acting advice as the shoot progressed, which has proved an invaluable boost to his on-screen offerings ever since. It comes as no surprise that, along with Jack Nicholson and Meg Ryan, he lists De Niro as one of his favourite screen stars.

Sadly, it was a dynamite combination which did little to boost the public interest. *This Boy's Life* was released in the US on April 23, 1993 – traditionally a quiet period at the US box office prior to the release of the all-conquering summer blockbuster season which would that year include the biggest film of all time *Jurassic Park*. The Spring release should, by rights, have given the movie a fighting chance, but the film disappeared from American cinemas after only a fortnight when the takings proved to be hugely disappointing – so much so, that *This Boy's Life* only secured a British release the following summer, and was given an extremely minor cinema outing before being sent swiftly to video. However, the small screen proved to be its saving grace, for the film received a much wider audience there than it had previously done at the pictures. If anything deterred prospective audiences, though, it must have been that the story was too depressing and moody for the thrill-seeking Saturday night crowds, because the film proved a smash hit with critics, many of whom rated *This Boy's Life* as one of the best films of the year. While Robert De Niro's performance received the inevitable plaudits, it was notable that the majority of the praise rested on the shoulders of his young co-star, many suggesting that his likeable, natural performance had completely stolen the show from the film's legendary lead.

Leonardo was praised by many reviewers for his outstanding performance as troubled teenager Toby. Such influential papers as the *Chicago Sun-Times* (with a write-up penned by hugely famous film critic Roger Ebert) and the *Washington Post* could not heap enough praise on Leonardo and the phrase 'the next big thing' began to be bandied about quite comfortably, while others lamented the fact that Tobias Wolff had not lived long enough to see himself portrayed so effectively onscreen.

Even trade bible *Variety* got in on the act, saying 'Centrescreen almost throughout, DiCaprio is excellent as Toby.'

When it finally made its appearance in the UK, to equally enthusiastic reviews, the attention was once again focused on Leonardo. Elsewhere, teenage magazines were giving the film the sort of coverage it could never have hoped for had it not been for the presence of its handsome young star. And DiCaprio was not forgotten when awards time came around, either. While the Oscar nomination remained unforthcoming, a trio of trophies came his way from the various groups of movie critics across America who give their own awards out every year.

For his performances in both *This Boy's Life*, and that of *What's Eating Gilbert Grape?*, Leonardo became the proud recipient of the New Generation Award from the Los Angeles Film Critics Association, the Chicago Film Critics honoured him with their Most Promising Actor accolade, and to top it all off nicely, a Best Supporting Actor runners-up prize came his way from both the New York Film Critics and the National Society of Film Critics. Leonardo DiCaprio had, in a very real sense, arrived.

Leonardo and Robert De Niro were to be reunited at a later date in the film *Marvin's Room*, the 1996 Oscar-nominated drama which received similar critical plaudits but made an equally lukewarm impact at the box office. But while *This Boy's Life* may have been dismissed as one of the many casualties that litter the cinemas every week, for Leonardo this particular effort was no flash in the pan.

The teen who once admitted that he wanted to be an actor because it would be a cool way for all the girls to notice him was getting attention for more than just his good looks. But while he could have taken the route of so many of his peers and chosen a more high-profile, handsome leading man role, his next outing proved to be a serious case of casting against type, a role which, like so many he has chosen since, gave his amazing acting talents a chance to shine through in full. The film in question was the highly original *What's Eating Gilbert Grape?*, and Oscar nomination was just a matter of months away.

Leonardo in reflective mode in *This Boy's Life* (above) and, opposite, in one of the films lighter moments

Grape Expectations

Leonardo takes on his most challenging role to date in *What's Eating Gilbert Grape?* – and is justly rewarded for his efforts

In choosing *What's Eating Gilbert Grape?* as his follow-up to *This Boy's Life*, Leonardo showed himself to be an actor who refused to be pigeonholed into heart-throb roles, choosing interesting films over surefire hits. It is a trait that he shared with his Gilbert Grape co-star, Johnny Depp, who had by this time made a name for himself in a string of arthouse and off-the-wall projects (*Benny And Joon*, *Arizona Dream* to name but two), most of which had garnered him ecstatic reviews but, with the exception of *Edward Scissorhands*, had gone virtually unnoticed by the cinema-going public.

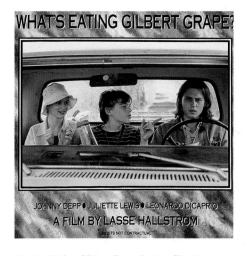

What's Eating Gilbert Grape? – the film that landed Leonardo a Best Supporting Actor nomination at the Oscars

What's Eating Gilbert Grape? is a quirky, often hilarious, and ultimately moving screen version of Peter Hedges' best-seller, directed by Swedish helmer Lasse Halstrom (previously best known for the 1970's classic *ABBA The Movie*). Johnny Depp stars as the title character, struggling to keep his head in a tiny town where everybody knows everybody else, and his dysfunctional family are somewhat infamous. Mom (Darlene Cates, who took up acting after being spotted on a talk show about agoraphobia) has ballooned to forty stone ever since their father hanged himself in the cellar, and is housebound; older sister Amy (Mary Kate Schellhardt) is put-upon, and duty bound to keep the family home together, and younger sister Ellen (Laura Harrington) is in the throes of adolescence and taking every teenage tantrum out on her unfortunate older brother.

DiCaprio, meanwhile, completes the family as Arnie, Gilbert's mentally handicapped sibling, who doctors said would not live to see the other side of ten. They were wrong. As the film opens, preparations are being made for Arnie's 18th birthday. While playful and well-meaning, Arnie's condition makes him highly uncontrollable; at one point he is arrested for climbing all the way to the top of the local TV tower, and baths become a thing of the past when he is accidentally left sitting in the tub all night. And when Gilbert is trying to impress visitor Becky (Juliette Lewis), by giving her a lift back to her caravan, Arnie, ever aware of his own impending death, attempts to make friends with the new arrival by informing her that 'I could go at any time . . .'

Although Leonardo did not have nearly such stiff competition when it came to the role of Arnie Grape as he had for that of Tobias Wolff, there were still obstacles to overcome, the main one being when he nearly lost out on the part altogether because he was considered by many to be far too handsome to play something which was so unglamorous. Fortunately, his looks proved not to be his downfall, and prior to filming he researched the role thoroughly by spending a great deal of time with other mentally handicapped people, in order to gain inspiration for Arnie's on-screen shenanigans.

The film itself was almost impossible to fault, with superb performances all round, but once again it was Leonardo's which really stood out, his research having paid off greatly. While Arnie was prone to the sort of behaviour that only a saint could fail to find fault with, Leonardo proved so affecting and vulnerable in the role that it proved impossible not to love him, no matter what he got up to. He was almost a little too convincing, as it happens; many viewers unfamiliar with Leonardo were

Leonardo, as the handicapped Arnie Grape visits the grave of his long-dead father

A Grape bonding session, in one of the films more poignant scenes

so taken in by his acting that they believed the part was being played by a genuinely handicapped teenager.

Like *This Boy's Life*, though, *Gilbert Grape* was similarly overlooked when it came to ticket sales. Released in the winter of 1993, some eight months after the former had made its quiet debut, critics couldn't praise the movie highly enough, and Leonardo once again found himself on the receiving end of plaudits a-plenty, (in one particularly memorable incident, screenwriter William Goldman declared 'Please don't let anything bad ever happen to Leonardo DiCaprio') but this time around there was a blockbuster season to contend with, and the spectacle of Robin Williams donning the latex to play Scottish nanny *Mrs. Doubtfire* was far more of a draw for the majority of moviegoers.

Still, *Gilbert Grape's* Christmas cinema outing did have one notable advantage attached to it; that of the impending awards season. Traditionally, the movies most likely to be noticed when it comes to Oscar nomina-

tions are released right at the end of the year, in order for them to be fresh in the memories of the voters, and *Gilbert Grape* proved to be no exception. Although the film was not quite strong enough to be featured in the Best Picture category (in a year which saw the likes of *Schindler's List* and *The Piano* going home laden down with new silverware), Leonardo's superb presence had captured the imagination of award-givers everywhere. In addition to the joint rewards critics had heaped upon him for both *This Boy's Life* and *Gilbert Grape* (see Chapter 2), he also copped a Golden Globe Nomination for Best Supporting Actor for the latter, and found himself attending his first major awards ceremony.

Leonardo may have gone home empty-handed, but there were greater things to come. The Golden Globes is always seen as an accurate pointer as to who will be short-listed come Oscar night, and sure enough, when the Academy Award nominations were announced, Leonardo found his name up there for his superb performance in *What's*

Eating Gilbert Grape?, sharing the list with such luminaries as Tommy Lee Jones (*The Fugitive*), Ben Kingsley (*Schindler's List*), Ralph Fiennes (*Schindler's List*) and Pete Postlethwaite (*In The Name Of The Father*). It was a memorable Oscar year – the year that Stephen Spielberg finally broke his Oscar duck, and youngest ever Oscar winner Anna Paquin (Best Supporting Actress for *The Piano*) stood on the stage speechless in front of a viewing audience of millions. And judging by the enormous cheer that went up in the auditorium when his name was read out, Leonardo was one of the most popular nominees of the night. However, the competition proved just too stiff, and he eventually lost out to Tommy Lee Jones for his performance as the cop chasing Harrison Ford in *The Fugitive*.

The fact that he had achieved all this by the age of 19, however, proved that Leonardo was turning into a force to be reckoned with, something which became apparent when *Gilbert Grape* was released elsewhere in the world and gained some much deserved success. Although his name was still not one of those which could open a film, he was reaching the stage where he could be picky about what he starred in, and so he did just that.

The local wild life leaves Arnie Grape completely undaunted

Left: Gilbert Grape's on screen family: L–R, Leonardo, Laura Harrington, Johnny Depp, Darlene Cates, and Mary Kate Schellhardt

Leonardo finds a sympathetic shoulder in onscreen brother Gilbert Grape (Johnny Depp)

While many stars would take the choice of the plum roles offered to them, Leonardo kept his artistic integrity intact and turned down a whole string of high-profile parts that would have made him a household name.

First up was *Hocus Pocus*, Disney's comedy about three witches (headed by Bette Midler) burned at the stake and returning to inflict their revenge on Halloween, only to be seen off by a kid far brainier than they. The role would not only have made Leonardo a good deal wealthier, but would also have provided him with that as yet elusive box office hit; *Hocus Pocus* eventually went ahead with ex-*Dallas* star Omri Katz taking the lead, and made a modest if unspectacular amount of money.

Far more lucrative, though, was the opportunity to play Robin in *Batman Forever*, the third part in the phenomenally successful franchise concentrating on the 90's adventures of the Caped Crusader. Again, Leonardo turned down the part which eventually went to Chris O'Donnell, and unsurprisingly, the film

went on to be the biggest grosser of 1995. O'Donnell, meanwhile, found himself rocketing into the megastar league and was so popular that he once again donned tights and mask for 1997's summer offering, *Batman And Robin*, together with George Clooney, the third actor to play the caped crimefighter in the series. Had Leonardo opted for the part, it would have seen him carrying the character into the next millennium (a fifth Bat-outing is already in the pipeline and more are being planned).

In addition, rumours began circulating that Leonardo was set for lead duties in a new biopic about James Dean, a troubled project which swung between directors for quite some time. In between all the production troubles, Leonardo eventually turned down the opportunity to star because he admitted 'I felt I wasn't experienced enough to play the part.' To this day, the movie remains uncast and no filming date has been set.

What Leonardo may have lacked in paycheques, however, he more than made up for

with a whole clutch of artistically satisfying projects, all of which had one thing in common; they all played upon the reputation he was gaining after *This Boy's Life* and *What's Eating Gilbert Grape?* for playing tortured, rebellious young things. It may have been an image at odds with his laid-back, happy life offscreen, but it was one he was seemingly more than happy to nurture in front of the camera.

Over the course of the next 18 months, he would gain attention from more than just the film reviewing press, becoming something of a gossip column staple in spite of his best attempts to keep his private life just that. The moviegoing millions, on the other hand would get to see him play the part of a tormented, drug addicted teenage poet in 20th Century America, a similarly unhappy, substance fuelled verse-scribbler in 18th Century France, and a reckless, rebellious gunslinger whose far from torturous existence would involve an onscreen kiss-up with Sharon Stone.

Leonardo's spectacular acting abilities branch out yet again

Leonardo at the 1994 Golden Globes with his Mum, Irmelin

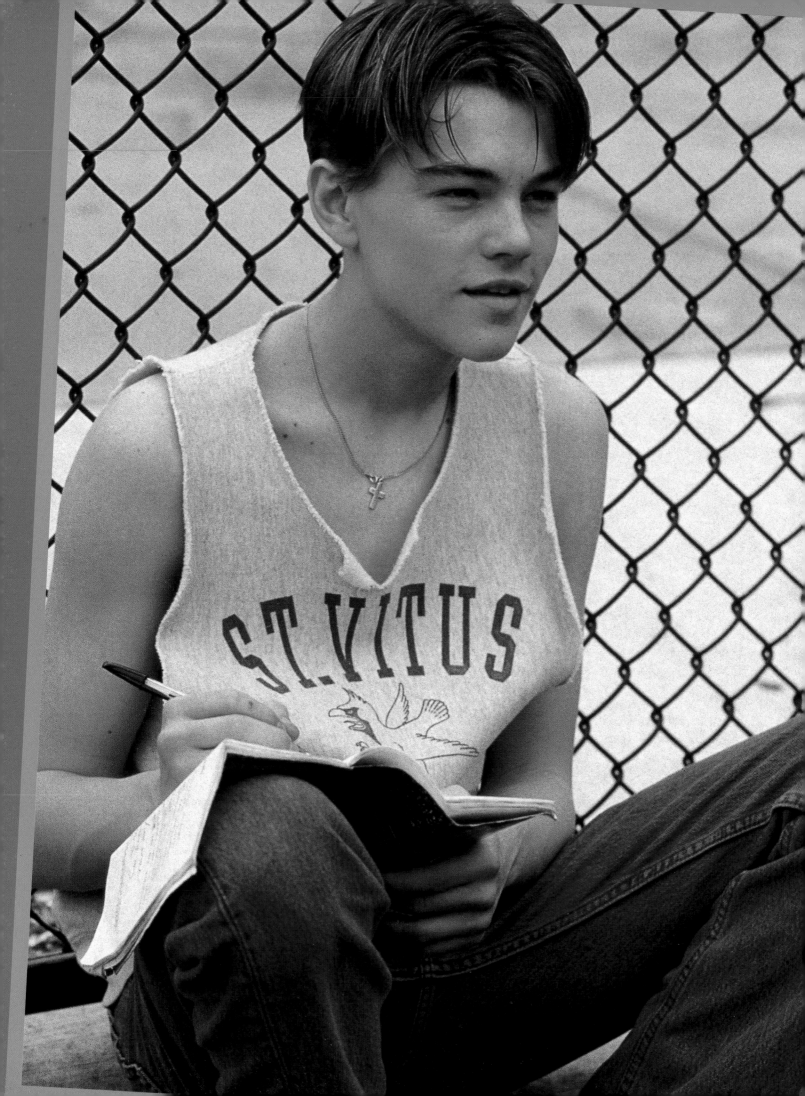

4

Guns, Girls and Drugs

Leonardo takes on a trio of thoroughly diverse roles

Leonardo landed yet another legendary onscreen dad – Gene Hackman

Opposite: Leonardo gave the other gunslingers a run for their money – but proved no match for Sharon Stone

*T*he Quick And The Dead, while not exactly a straightforward blockbuster, was the closest that Leonardo had yet come to appearing in a commercial project, largely due to the fact that he would be co-starring alongside the likes of Sharon Stone and Gene Hackman. In fact, it was entirely down to Sharon that he landed the role in the film at all, with the *Basic Instinct* siren having been so impressed by his previous work that she personally hand-picked him for the role of The Kid in the offbeat Western.

Directed by Sam Raimi, previously best known for such notorious horror flicks as *The Evil Dead*, *The Quick And The Dead* stars Sharon as a mysterious woman coming to a no-name town to seek revenge (for what, exactly, gradually becomes clear throughout the course of the movie) through a series of gun battles which involve her knocking off the majority of the grizzled stetson-wearers in the

Leonardo looking his coolest in *The Quick And The Dead*

town. Eventually the duels come to rest with a trio of figures – sheriff Herod (Gene Hackman), who obviously knows more about the woman than he's letting on, the man she has unexpectedly fallen for (played by Australian actor Russell Crowe) and The Kid, Herod's son, who is so keen to impress his grizzled father that he pretends to be far more of a gunslinging hero than he actually is.

Leonardo gets to enjoy himself enormously in the role, as a teenager basking in bravado, who can't wait to beat Sharon at her own game and spends most of the film talking about his prowess with a gun and messing around with bigger and bigger weapons. Unsurprisingly, most of it is just talk, and come the inevitable showdown with Sharon, it's a very different story. By this time, though, Leonardo has won over the audience by being the only character, aside from the leading lady, with a shred of humanity, although given the huge amount of comic book violence going on left, right and centre, it's impossible to take anybody too seriously.

This was, for the most part, the closest Leonardo had come to a comic performance – the movie was very humorous in tone and gave him the chance to swagger around talking tough in hugely impressive fashion while still retaining the mixed-up young man characteristics that had seen him through his career thus far. It did, in short, prove his versatility, at the same time equipping him with such fresh skills as horse-riding. On a more personal level, the media had begun to sit up and take notice of Leonardo, with his name beginning to creep around the gossip columns. Sharon Stone's admiration for the young actor proved so public that the pair were, naturally, romantically linked, rumours which proved to be unfounded. As it happens, the closest the pair did come to locking lips was sharing an onscreen kiss, and he was less than enamoured. 'It wasn't that great actually,' he later said of having to pucker up to his co-star. 'She grabbed me by the hair and pushed her lips against mine and then threw my head away. It was by no means a real kiss.'

Real or otherwise, it did nothing to help the box office performance of the film, which was released in the States the Autumn of 1994 to decidedly negative reviews and vanished from cinemas very quickly. The bizarre on-screen goings-on fared far better outside of the US, although Leonardo emerged from proceedings relatively unscathed, having garnered his fair share of acclaim on both sides of the Atlantic and was seen by many as the high point of the film. While his credibility was still intact, the all-important box office hit was still proving elusive.

Nor was it to prove forthcoming with his next batch of projects. Before embarking upon what would be his most intense role to date, Leonardo made a tiny appearance in a little-seen French production, *Une Cent Et Une Nuits* (One Hundred And One Nights). Billed only on the credits as Furtive And Friendly Appearance – Leonardo DiCaprio, the film itself centred on an ailing 100-year-old man whose nurse eases his suffering by telling him stories about all the movies ever made, while a bunch of student movie makers try to sponge cash off the centenarian for their own film-producing ends. Fellow Furtive and Friendly cameos came from the likes of

teen star Stephen Dorff and Gallic mega-star Gerard Depardieu, and an entire galaxy of stars, including Harrison Ford and Emily Lloyd, turn up under alternate guises. Given that the film was more of an ensemble piece featuring tiny cameos from all the above talent, Leonardo's appearance never attracted a great deal of attention.

Equally bizarre was a low-budget short film, *The Foot Shooting Party*, which saw Leonardo as a rock star being drafted for war. A black and white effort, it was most notable for the fact that it featured the man himself sporting hair extensions, although it still drifted by largely unnoticed, so much so that most people don't even realise Leonardo starred in it.

However, the same could not be said of his next outing, *The Basketball Diaries*. Based on the life of teen poet Jim Carroll, whose fondness for shooting hoops was nothing compared to his love of shooting heroin, the role required an actor who would be able to go from being the fresh face of the school basketball team, experimenting with drugs out of teenage curiosity, through a drug-hungry addict disowned by his mother and living in a filthy squat, through to, ultimately, a horrifying

L–R, Mark Wahlberg, Leonardo and James Hadid starring in *The Basketball Diaries*

Leonardo with sultry *Basketball Diaries* co-star
Brittany Daniel

and deeply unpleasant withdrawal scene. Until Leonardo came along, the project had been lingering on the shelf for some time, because the producers had been unable to find an actor who would be able to convey such a wide range of emotions so powerfully. However, once he appeared on the scene, they knew they had found their Jim Carroll.

The Basketball Diaries is, as might be expected, a grim movie experience which, while fascinating, is devoid of any humour or respite and as such hardly makes for a cosy night's viewing. But Leonardo's performance saves the day, whether he is scribbling poetry, having one of many conflicts with his onscreen mother (Lorraine Bracco) or indulging in an almighty drug-taking session with his friends. The film also marked the first major screen appearance of Mark Wahlberg (aka former pop star Marky Mark) who does an impressive job as Jim's sleazy best friend, the one responsible for his addiction in the first place.

Making the movie proved to be no easy task. While Leonardo's life long love of basketball (it is his favourite sport) stood him in good stead for the hoop-shooting scenes, the onscreen drug activity proved to be a different story. He spent several weeks prepping himself for the pivotal withdrawal scene and afterwards said of the experience 'it required me to achieve a primal state of being – I had to turn into an animal almost.' The results speak

Leonardo and Mark Wahlberg at *The Basketball Diaries* premiere

for themselves, with Leonardo turning in an astoundingly convincing performance in the scene in question. 'I don't like what drugs do,' he later confessed. 'I don't do anything except drink once in a while.'

But what really brought him to public attention was his behaviour off-set. While shooting, *The Basketball Diaries* in New York, Leonardo was rarely out of the tabloids for long thanks to his party animal activities, having been spotted at some of the Big Apple's hottest nightclubs on a number of occasions, with a string of different women, from actress Juliette Lewis (who appeared with Leonardo in *What's Eating Gilbert Grape?*) through to *Clueless* starlet Alicia Silverstone and teen supermodel Bridget Hall (best known for her modelling contract with designer Ralph Lauren).

As well as all the obvious romantic links, he was even linked to a couple of brawls in the aforementioned clubs. But while Leonardo admits he would much rather go out and party than remain 'cooped up in his hotel room', he is the first to point out that the majority of the reports were worryingly over-exaggerated, and that the fights were very much a figment of the tabloids' imagination. 'Bridget and I hung out for all of a week,' he later pointed out, 'the whole thing was totally blown out of proportion.'

The Basketball Diaries, on the other hand, didn't get quite the same amount of publicity, and despite Leonardo's performance getting the usual raves, the movie proved just too dark for mainstream cinema audiences and consequently went the way of all his other cinema outings. It performed marginally better outside of the US, although the British video release was marred due to a scene in which Jim Carroll dreams that he goes into his classroom with a shotgun and massacres his fellow pupils. As the small screen release was due just a couple of weeks after the Dunblane tragedy, the offending footage was appropriately removed.

Leonardo's next foray into the film world was an equally gloomy affair. *Total Eclipse* was a biopic based around the precocious 18th Century French poet Rimbaud, whose musings about life came to a swift end when he died at the age of 19. The crux of the film was his homosexual relationship with fellow verse-scribbler Verlaine (played by British actor David Thewlis), and the wild, largely opium-fuelled lifestyle that the pair of them led.

It seemed ironic that Leonardo should play two poets in a row, given that he is something of a scribe himself, and spends much of his offscreen time writing his own verse. Even more coincidentally, the part, which was originally meant to be taken by River Phoenix (with John Malkovich as Verlaine) became his after the former's tragic death. It was not the first time that Leonardo had gone up for a part vacated by River, as he was all set to play the crucial journalist hearing out Brad Pitt's 200-year-old tale in *Interview With The Vampire* –

Leonardo is re-united with Sharon Stone at the 1995 Oscars

until that was bagged by Christian Slater. This time around, he was luckier. Jim Carroll, the writer he had played in *The Basketball Diaries*, actually suggested that he audition for Rimbaud, and it marked a major departure for Leonardo – not only did the script call for him to play a homosexual love scene, but also for him to appear nude, something he had never done before. Typically, he was entirely unfazed by it all, joking about the scene in question, in particular his judicious use of mouthwash beforehand.

Unfortunately, the film was his most poorly received yet, not even getting a theatrical release in some countries until two years after it was completed. Leonardo did, as usual, escape relatively unscathed, but many critics found the movie just too pretentious and dull for their liking, and unsurprisingly, the public stayed away.

Had Leonardo taken the *Batman Forever* route, he would no doubt have become a superstar by this point. But the fringe benefits of film stardom soon became apparent. He moved out of his mother's home into a swanky Los Angeles pad, which he now shares with his bizarre pet, a bearded dragon lizard, and a music collection that ranges from Pink Floyd to The Beatles and Led Zeppelin (he is also a big fan of rap music). He swapped his former set of wheels for a silver BMW Coupe. And, he began to find that despite the lack of box office success, he was able to pick and choose just whatever scripts came landing on his doorstep.

Fortunately, Leonardo's next choice was not only a classic story, but finally provided him with that long-awaited box office smash. With period drama very much in vogue, thanks to the successful adaptation of Jane Austen's novels for the big screen, it seemed that the next writer to be dusted down and revived was Shakespeare – and with *Richard III* and Kenneth Branagh's four-hour *Hamlet* already on their way, it would only be a matter of time before the world's most timeless tale of star-crossed lovers followed them back into cinemas. *Romeo And Juliet* had been filmed before, it was true – but never quite like this. And if anybody had any doubts that Leonardo DiCaprio was heading for star status, this particular effort would change their minds.

Leonardo, David Thewlis and some fetching period costumes in *Total Eclipse*

20th Century Romeo

Shakespeare gets a shake-up and Leonardo gets a hit movie

Leonardo DiCaprio is a self-confessed romantic. 'When I'm alone with a girl, I can really get into the whole baby voices, rubbing noses – the teddy bear thing.' He has fond memories of his first date, with a girl named Cessi, who he spent the entire summer falling in love with over a series of lengthy phone conversations. 'Then she came home, and we met to go out for the first time, to the movies (the film in question being *When Harry Met Sally*). When I saw her I was so petrified I couldn't even look her in the eye.' Inevitably, the date went so disastrously wrong that the girl he had once been so keen on avoided him for months afterwards.

However, all of this stood him in good stead when he opted to play one half of the most famous romantic couple in the whole of literary history – the innocent lovestruck teenager Romeo in *William Shakespeare's Romeo And Juliet*, a role which required him to be both passionate and struck dumb at the sight of his first love. The adaptation in question promised to be quite unlike any screen version of the play so far – the last production, filmed in 1969 before Leonardo had even been born, was a largely traditional affair.

In the hands of Australian helmer Baz Luhrmann, on the other hand, it was a different story. The director, whose last film had been the wildly original comedy *Strictly Ballroom*, went for a thoroughly modern spin on things. The story – together with most of

Romeo And Juliet turned Leonardo's name into a household one

Opposite: *Romeo And Juliet* **had critics everywhere in raptures**

43

the dialogue – has remained intact. Romeo and Juliet, for the uninitiated, are a pair of star-crossed lovers who fall head over heels for one another, even though their families are sworn enemies, woo each other from the latter's balcony, marry in secret and suffer the consequences when Romeo's best friend is killed and he ends up going on a vengeful spree that leads to him being banished from the town. Meanwhile, Juliet is being forced into a marriage she doesn't want to a nice but-oh-so-boring suitor, Paris, and is offered an escape method by a local priest so she can be with her new husband once again, but naturally it all goes horribly wrong and ends tragically.

What distinguished this particular *Romeo And Juliet*, however, was its setting. Originally taking place in the Italian city of Verona, the action now switches to the decidedly Los Angelean Verona Beach, with the opposing families taking the form of gangs who speed around in cars all day waging gun battles

against each other. Mercutio, the doomed best friend of Romeo, makes his initial appearance in a sequinned bra and hotpants number, and when Romeo and Juliet meet for the first time, they glimpse each other through a giant tank full of tropical fish. All this against a fantastic soundtrack featuring the likes of Garbage and The Cardigans, and an ending far more heartbreaking than any adaptation which has gone before it.

It seemed, in a way, that the part of Romeo could have been written for Leonardo, so perfect was he as the lovelorn one. As per usual, he seemed very much to play up the tortured young man side of things – when we first meet him, he is wandering the beach lamenting an unrequited love and looking thoroughly sorry for himself. Initially, he was reluctant to help bring the oft-filmed story to the screen yet again. 'My instinctive reaction was why do another one? There didn't seem to be a reason.' However, once he had travelled to Australia to meet with Baz Luhrmann, and

Leonardo, as Romeo, avenges the death of best friend Mercutio

20th Century Romeo

found out about the new interpretation for himself, his mind was soon changed. 'I realised it was a little more hard-core and a lot cooler,' he said afterwards. 'I certainly wouldn't have done it if I'd had to jump around in tights. But Baz Luhrmann heightened a lot of things in the story, made it kind of a futuristic fantasy world that made it a lot easier for people around my age to identify with the story. It wasn't just about *Romeo And Juliet* any more.'

The female half of the smitten couple, meanwhile, was played by young actress Claire Danes, an up-and-coming star who, like Leonardo, has been hailed as the finest new talent of her generation. At just 17, she has already accumulated roles in a whole host of movies with some of Hollywood's biggest names, starring as Winona Ryder's sickly sister in *Little Women*, playing Holly Hunter's daughter in *Home For The Holidays* and having the ghost of Michelle Pfeiffer as her mother in *To Gillian On Her 37th Birthday*. However, Claire is to date best known as

philosophical teen Angela Chase on the hugely popular TV series *My So-Called Life*, which has also brought her co-star Jared Leto to the attention of an adoring public. Amazingly, some people thought that Leonardo looked younger than his elfin co-star, despite the fact that he is five years her senior (she was 16, he 21 at the time of filming). But his boyish looks have always been an advantage for Leonardo, allowing him to play characters many years younger than himself and give them added depth thanks to his experience. Rounding out the cast were Hispanic actor John Leguizamo (best known for *Super Mario Brothers* and *To Wong Foo*), and British thesps Pete Postlethwaite and Miriam Margolyes.

Filming, meanwhile, entailed an arduous three-month stint in Mexico City, a place which the cast and crew found was frequently fraught with danger. While in South America, Leonardo cemented his status as a party animal once and for all, heading the cast in local parties, late-night board game sessions in

It can only be a matter of time before it all turns tragic

Leonardo hangs out with *Romeo And Juliet* director Baz Luhrmann

his hotel room and, on more than one occasion, checking out the nearby nightclubs. On one particularly bizarre night, things turned sour as one of Leonardo's friends, visiting from LA, was beaten up by a nightclub bouncer in an apparently motiveless attack, while trying to get into the club that his famous friend was already in. Across town, even weirder goings-on were afoot, as one of the film's crew members, upon hailing a taxi to return home from another club, was involved in a violent car-jacking that resulted in him being kidnapped, robbed and ultimately hospitalized. 'Loads of crazy things happened out there,' Leonardo later recalled. 'Four people (not involved with the film) from our hotel got murdered.'

And as if that wasn't enough, illness reared its head as well, with Leonardo, Claire and director Baz Luhrmann all going down with Montezuma's Revenge (a form of dysentery) which put them all out of action for at least a week. None of this, however, put paid to the star's natural exuberance which, as ever, shone through on set. Between takes he would bide his time running circuits of the set, dancing around to his beloved hip-hop music, doing Michael Jackson impersonations, and

interspersing them with similar take-offs of cast members just as they strode in front of the camera to do their bit. In short, he was very much the centre of attention, not least from the local girls who came down to watch the shoot. But once he was called on set to do his bit, he had no trouble behaving himself and delivering the goods. And his disruptive behaviour is shrugged off by most of the directors he has worked with as part of his creative process. Leonardo is quick to explain: 'I would have a nervous breakdown if I had to be a character for three months on and off set. I know what I'm doing, but when they say Cut, I'm fine. I don't hide in a corner and yell at anyone who tries to speak to me. I don't want to become a strange person, or give up the life I already have.'

Nor, for that matter, did Leonardo appear phased by the goings on in Mexico City. 'It was an extraordinary place,' he says, 'We had fantastic places to use, the churches, the backdrops and the people added to the elements we wanted to use in the movie. But I think that being in a place like that, which was really dangerous – the actors kind of stuck around each other and developed a good tight bond.'

Romeo And Juliet; don't try this one at home

That first meeting; Leonardo as Romeo peeps through the fish tank and claps eyes on Juliet

Something which did, of course, spark off the inevitable rumours that Leonardo and Claire had become romantically entwined for real during the shoot, especially given the astonishing onscreen chemistry which set reports had suggested they were generating. However, such allegations were swiftly scotched, with him laying claim to a non-showbiz girlfriend whom he had been dating for some time, and her long-term involvement with rock musician Andrew Dorff, younger brother of *Backbeat* star Stephen. (The pair have since parted company). In fact, there were times, especially towards the end of filming, when things became quite fraught between the two of them. But after the numerous traumas they had experienced together, by the end the pair had formed a close bond, and were behaving like brother and sister.

Romeo And Juliet, meanwhile, made its debut US outing on November 1, 1996, following an energetic summer which had seen Leonardo trying his hand at the riskiest white knuckle sports going – white water rafting,

bungee jumping and even a parachute jump. The first two were just fine, but the skydiving nearly ended in disaster after the star's parachute failed to open, leaving him free-falling thousands of feet until the backup chute was able to inflate. Far safer, if no less scary, was the second leg of the vacation, which saw him taking in some of Los Angeles's best theme parks – he claims to have visited Knott's Berry Farm, Magic Mountain, Raging Waters and Universal Studios three times each in the space of only a couple of months.

His next public appearance was at the American premiere of *Romeo And Juliet*, at which he revealed just where his romantic interests lay, showing up arm-in-arm with model Kristin Zang. Although Leonardo is renowned for keeping his private life private, it soon became apparent that the pair had already been an item for around a year. Indeed, Leonardo's fondness for fashion shows is one of the reasons why he has become such a tabloid favourite over the past couple of years.

Most notably, *Romeo And Juliet* helped to drag Leonardo out of his undeserved box office slump. Against some fantastic reviews, the film shot to the top of the US box office, making over $14 million in its first weekend on release and bringing Shakespeare to audiences who had never previously considered it. In particular, the film reached a large teenage audience, who lapped up its young, sexy, MTV-style approach to its subject matter. In the end, the film grossed around $50 million in the US and was a similar success in other parts of the world.

Even more importantly, *Romeo And Juliet* established its leading man as a force to be reckoned with. Many talked of a second Oscar nomination for Leonardo, but when Academy Awards time rolled around, the film was mentioned only in the technical categories. This didn't stop it snagging its much deserved acclaim elsewhere though, and at the Berlin Film Festival the following February Leonardo was the proud recipient of the Silver Bear Award for Best Actor for that very film. What's more, *Romeo And Juliet* was not overlooked when the MTV Movie Awards rolled around either, with the film copping six nominations, including Best Male Performance for Leonardo and Best Female Performance for Claire Danes, as well as Best Fight Sequence and Best Movie, which pitted it against such stiff competition as *Scream* and *Independence Day*.

By now, there can have been absolutely no doubt in anybody's mind that Leonardo DiCaprio had arrived. His acting talents were up there on screen for all to see, his face adorned many a teenager's wall and, to top it all off nicely, he finally had a hit film in the bag. He even began building his mother a home in West Virginia, far away from the sleazy Hollywood suburb where he had grown up. But rather than capitalise on the success of *Romeo And Juliet*, his next film saw him returning to the low-key affairs of old, a movie which not only re-united him with Robert De Niro but also allowed him to work with the likes of Diane Keaton and Meryl Streep. It was merely a temporary move, however, for it was only going to be a matter of months before he found himself taking the lead in one of the most expensive movies ever to go before a camera. The film in question was James Cameron's *Titanic*, and the hype machine had been set in motion before a reel of film had even been shot.

Romeo and Mercutio (Harold Perrineau) gear up for another battle

The women in Leonardo's life; Mother Irmelin and model girlfriend Kristen Zang

6

Maiden Voyage

Marvin's Room and *Titanic* pave the way for further glory

Long before *Romeo And Juliet* achieved hit status, Leonardo had already made up his mind what his next move would be – and, none too surprisingly, it was playing yet another disturbed teenager in a low-budget outing. Coincidentally, it was another movie whose origins lay in play form – although *Marvin's Room*, unlike *Romeo And Juliet*, was of considerably low profile, known only to those who had caught the hit off-Broadway production.

Although the role itself was only a supporting one, *Marvin's Room* would give Leonardo the opportunity to work with such Hollywood royalty as Meryl Streep and Diane Keaton, as well as being reunited with Robert de Niro. The film is a low-key affair about sisters Lee and Bessie, the former (Meryl Streep) is a brassy hairdresser who has long since legged it to the big city to raise her two sons, Hank (Leonardo) and Charlie (Hal Scardino) leaving her gentle, sweet-natured older sibling (Diane Keaton) to look after their ever-ageing relatives back home. However, she returns home, sons in tow, for the inevitable reconciliation, when Bessie is diagnosed as having leukaemia. Thus a whole string of familial conflict is played out, with things coming to a head on a disastrous trip to Disneyworld (giving Leonardo the chance to take in the one theme park he didn't make it to on his summer vacation).

Even though Leonardo's part in the film was only a small one, it was of great significance. His character, Hank, is a 17-year-old juvenile delinquent forever in and out of correctional institutions, but as might be expected, it all boils down to the abusive, tragic time he had as a kid and suggests that his character may ultimately have the chance to make good after all.

Naturally, he did a grand job on screen, winning the admiration of the legendary figures he found himself up against with his laid-back attitude and an assured performance which was on the receiving end of much critical praise in spite of the mixed reviews the film received.

Many suggested that the acting was infinitely superior to the film itself, something which became largely apparent when Diane Keaton received a Best Actress nomination at that year's Oscars (Leonardo was, sadly, overlooked when it came to awards time, although this may not be such a bad thing, given that he has since expressed relief that he did not win the Oscar for *Gilbert Grape*). However, the accolade did have the knock-on effect of giving Leonardo his second box office hit in a row, with *Marvin's Room* getting a major rally as a result, and making enough money to be classed a surprise success.

Having wrapped that particular project, rumours once again began to circulate about whose camera Leonardo would decide to jump behind next. The strongest of these had him being wooed by legendary director Francis Ford Coppola for his adaptation of *The Rainmaker*, based on the novel by super-author John Grisham – a mainstream blockbuster that would be assured hit status. Although, the helmsman was on the lookout for an up and coming young talent, he eventually settled on newcomer Matt Damon and, ironically, Claire Danes. But the man who had been shunning commercially viable sure things left, right and centre, finally settled on a film touted as one of the biggest blockbusters for many a year, a movie which would not only cost a great deal and receive more publicity than any other production that year, but would finally give its star the chance to play a grown-up – and a relatively happy one at that.

Already prompting 'most expensive film of all time' talk thanks to its reported $200 million

Opposite: Yet another disturbed teen role for Leonardo, this time as Meryl Streep's son in *Marvin's Room*

RYL STREEP   LEONARDO DICAPRIO   DIANE KEATON   and   ROBERT DE NIRO

A story about the years
that keep us apart...
And the moments
that bring us together.

MARVIN'S ROOM

price tag, the movie in question is *Titanic*, the latest effort from James Cameron. Although the director is best known for such superb action outings as *Terminator 1* and *2* and the Arnold Schwarzenegger barnstormer *True Lies*, *Titanic* is a very different affair – an epic romance set aboard the doomed cruise liner which sank in 1912 on its maiden outing, killing 1512 of those on board. The topic itself spent most of the year basking in renewed popularity, but even though a *Titanic* stage musical opened just a few months beforehand, it's far from three plays to films in a row for Leonardo – this time around, the only thing the projects have in common is their subject matter.

The set-up has Leonardo as free-spirited artist Jack Dawson, a third-class traveller on the ship who unexpectedly meets first-class voyager Rose De Witt Bukater (played by British actress Kate Winslet, best-known for her Oscar-nominated turn as Emma Thompson's younger sister in *Sense And Sensibility*) when he saves her life after a botched suicide attempt. The 17-year-old is trying to end it all because she feels stifled by her upper-crust upbringing and engagement to wealthy older man Cal Hockley (Billy Zane); however, when she happens upon Jack, the pair embark on a torrid romance, which is only scuppered by the unfortunate sinking of the ship.

The action flits back and forth between these events and the present day, where a bounty hunter (Bill Paxton) is preparing to go underwater to check out the remnants for himself, and discovers a sketch of Rose lovingly created by Jack Dawson, in which she is wearing a hugely valuable long-lost diamond heirloom. Subsequently, the now 100-year-old Rose, who survived the sinking (played by veteran actress Gloria Stuart) is called in to try and prevent opportunists from snatching the gem – a 56-carat necklace known as The Heart Of The Ocean – for themselves, all the while reminiscing about her experiences on the ship.

Leonardo, fresh from *Marvin's Room*, came aboard the project in May of 1996, and filming, which began the following August and

Jack Dawson (Leonardo) shows the lovely Rose DeWitt Bukater (played by Kate Winslett) his portfolio on A-deck in the mega-movie *Titanic*

Yet another legendary co-star for Leonardo – this time Diane Keaton in *Marvin's Room*

lasted for eight months, two months longer than originally scheduled, once again saw Leonardo heading off to Mexico, as well as San Diego and Escondido in California, and the remote Canadian island of Nova Scotia. This time it was to Rosarito Beach, where a replica of the ship had been built that was around 700 feet long – only 182 feet shy of the size of the original. To prevent the extra expense of having to film at sea, the model was built within a giant tank which was filled with millions of gallons of water, giving passers-by the impression that it really was ocean-bound.

So far, Leonardo has said very little about his experiences on the film, leaving most of the talking to Kate Winslet and James Cameron. '*Titanic* is a whole new adventure for me,' he has admitted, however, 'I've never gone to something this commercial before. It's good for me to be doing something like this – and, of course, it's a love story.' What is known is that his character underwent a name change early on from James to Jack, that the ending, originally set to provide Leonardo's fans with a quadruple hanky opportunity, may have been altered to something altogether happier, and that the shoot itself was anything but plain sailing.

The film's first bout of publicity came about at a pre-shooting party thrown in Nova Scotia, which saw several members of the cast and crew taken ill after consuming lobster chowder that somebody had spiked with the hallucinogenic drug PCP. James Cameron and Bill Paxton were among those affected, although Leonardo was not – it still remains unclear whether he was even at the party to begin with.

Far more gruelling for the star were the many scenes filmed on or below the water – one of which almost ended in tragedy. It involved Leonardo and Kate running along the deck of the ship to avoid being deluged by a giant wave – only to be confronted by a closed gate. Having managed to open it, however, Kate became trapped when her coat became snagged and the weight of her costume dragged her beneath the water. Only by squeezing out of the item in question did she manage to save herself from drowning. Other scenes saw Leonardo actually being dunked in the water himself, as the twosome attempt to swim to safety after the sinking of the ship

Leonardo in *Marvin's Room* with co-star Meryl Streep as his hairdresser Mum

– although this particular part of the shoot was saved till the very last day. It was hardly the easiest piece of acting in the world to end on, given that Leonardo and Kate, along with the hundreds of crew members, had been required to work 19 hour days much of the time – given that the Titanic sank at night, a great deal of the action could not be filmed until it was dark, meaning that Leonardo's partying had to be put on hold for a while. Also, a number of accidents were reported, with one stunt double breaking his arm in a fall, and one of the many extras being laid up with a broken leg after skidding on the deck.

And naturally, the gossip columnists had a field day, reports running rife that Leonardo and Kate had become an item in spite of his now public relationship with Kristen Zang. The stories were swiftly scotched though, as with Claire Danes in *Romeo And Juliet*, the intensity of the shoot resulted in the two leads forging a close friendship, and the latter later said that her co-star was a joy to work with.

During filming, meanwhile, Leonardo found himself on the receiving end of yet another sought-after accolade, when best-selling American magazine *People* published their annual list of The 50 Most Beautiful People In The World – and he was on it. Citing the magnetic effect he seemed to have on women, especially while on the sets of *Romeo And Juliet* and *Titanic*, Leonardo was quoted in a later interview as being unable to comprehend what all the fuss was about. 'Suddenly all these teenage girls have become hysterical,' he pointed out, 'and some of the things they do – climbing over walls and stuff are shocking'.

Even with the presence of its very own beautiful person, quite how *Titanic* will turn out still remains a mystery – although those who have read the script have said that it is a dead cert for gong status come the 1998 Oscars. However, with James Cameron still hard at work in the editing suite as the release date drew ever closer (the first cut of the film reportedly ran for over five hours), together with a great deal of talk about the ever-ballooning budget, (Cameron apparently waived his own fee in order to bring the costs down to a more manageable level, although the final total is still set to come in at around the $175 million mark), rumour started to spread that

Titanic would not be ready in time to set sail in cinemas over the summer, with conflicting reports that it would make its debut any time from Thanksgiving up until Christmas.

After much banter, including a much publicised outburst from Harrison Ford, furious that a change in *Titanic's* summer arrival would coincide with his own seasonal blockbuster *Air Force One*, the release date was eventually switched to December 19 in the USA, thus securing an early 1998 outing in other parts of the world. However, any suggestion that the film would not have been completed in time to land on shores in the late summer was swiftly denied, with studio chiefs pointing out that releasing it at the holiday season would give it a better chance of turning a profit. And with the running time coming in at the three hour mark, a lengthy peek at *Titanic's* star is most certainly on the cards, but those eagerly awaiting the event will have to be content to spend summer glimpsing the – reportedly magnificent – four-minute trailer to be distributed to cinemas over said months to whet the appetites of moviegoers. In other words, Leonardo's fans' chances of seeing him in a movie in the summer of 1997 may have diminished, but it isn't all doom and gloom, as a later release could well prove to be advantageous – as the movies which are the prime candidates for awards glory tend to be released towards the latter end of the year, the change in date could hugely help Leonardo's chances of having to prepare an acceptance speech. And, if nothing else, his presence in the movie should secure his status as a household name. 'Although you never know what's going to happen' he philosophically points out, 'because one season you're hot, the next you're cold. And you have to hold on to who you are, because the press is a powerful influence.'

Whatever the outcome, though, *Titanic* was certainly worth the wait, be it for the impressive special effects (underwater footage of an extensive nature is promised) or, for Leonardo lovers, the chance to see him in his very first totally mainstream outing. In addition, the troublesome shoot doesn't seem to have stopped him being thoroughly prolific, and with a trio of very different projects all about to make their mark, the future looks incredibly bright.

Jack (Leonardo) joins Rose (Kate Winslett) for dinner as a reward for 'saving her life' in a scene from *Titanic*.

7

France and Beyond

Leonardo during a promotional trip for *The Basketball Diaries*

As if filming *Titanic* didn't prove energetic enough, Leonardo was the first to disembark, in order to spend the summer of 1997 swashbuckling his way through another big budget offering – the period adventure *The Man In The Iron Mask.* Based on a character by *Three Musketeers* penner Alexandre Dumas, and with swordplay authentically lensing in Paris, *The Man In the Iron Mask* marks a string of firsts for Leonardo – not only is it the first time he has actually played a character in a bygone era and costume (he will, indeed, be sporting tights), but cinemagoers will also be greeted with Leonardo in dual roles, one of which sees him on debut villain duties. He plays both the scheming 18th Century monarch Louis XIV, and the titular hero who is imprisoned by said king. The latter's identity remains a constant mystery, and although he is also played by Leonardo, his face remains encased in a mask for the majority of the movie, but fortunately the Three Musketeers come to his rescue, in the shape of Jeremy Irons, John Malkovich and Gerard Depardieu. As might be expected, Leonardo jumped at the chance to add such names to his ever-expanding roster of co-stars.

And while in France, the party animal in him emerged once again – this time at a mammoth bash thrown at the 50th Cannes Film Festival to celebrate the opening of a new branch of Planet Hollywood in the town. As well as Sylvester Stallone, Bruce Willis and Demi Moore (co-owners along with Arnold Schwarzenegger) showing up to celebrate, Leonardo was one of the many invited guests, largely due to his close friendship with Bruce and Demi.

It is projects such as *The Man In The Iron Mask* and *Titanic* which are making Leonardo's status as an A-list fixture look assured. Now, with a little help from his script-scanning father, he can pick and choose whatever he happens to like the look of, while big name producers are queuing up to use his astonishing acting talents for themselves.

True to form, though, Leonardo's super-star standing has not prevented him from taking on roles in the smaller, more interesting projects which shaped his career in the first place. One such effort is *Don's Plum*, a low-budget American independent which centres around a young, up-and-coming cast fronted by Leonardo (and also including promising young actor Tobey Maguire.) It's an ensemble piece, which centres around one night in the life of a group of twenty-something buddies, and is event-packed stuff, even though the majority of the action takes place in the same

Leonardo still takes Mum Irmelin to many a showbiz gathering

67

coffee bar. Apart from Leonardo, *Don's Plum* has the added selling point of being shot in black and white – an ambitious move, and not the first time Leonardo has been involved with such a project (the short film *The Foot Shooting Party* was also a monochrome affair). Even further afield is *Slay The Dreamer*, a thriller based on the events surrounding the assassination of Dr. Martin Luther King Jr. in 1968, and starring Leonardo as idealistic young lawyer Jeffrey Jenkins. In what could be his most grown-up role to date, Leonardo's character becomes more involved in the killing than he could have possibly imagined, when his views draw him into a powerful confrontation with his father, who may just know more than he's letting on. Also making an appearance is *Pulp Fiction* star Samuel L Jackson as the Rev James Lawson, whose investigation into the assassination forms the backbone of the movie.

But even as Leonardo remains impossibly busy, so the rumour mill continues to churn. If stories are correct, he has enough film outings planned to keep him busy right into the next millennium – although the only one which looks as though it may come to fruition is the long-talked about movie adaptation of Jack Kerouac's novel *On The Road*, a 1950s set yarn which would provide Leonardo with a role every bit as offbeat as the ones which he has become accustomed to playing.

But whichever path his career may take, it looks certain that he will remain unaffected by fame. He may drive around in a starry BMW Coupe, but the interior doesn't exactly scream star treatment, with bubble gum wrappers, CDs, and $5 pairs of sunglasses littering the back seat. He may have moved away from the slums where he spent the earlier part of his life, but Leonardo is happiest having his feet kept firmly on the ground by his non-showbiz pals from his pre-stardom days. The only part of his fame he does appear to take advantage of is getting things for free – be it the latest pair of designer trainers or party tickets, Leonardo is quick to confess that it is one perk of his job he is fond of.

However, if there's one place other than the multiplexes where Leonardo has made an enormous impact, it's the Internet. One of the biggest crazes of recent years is for movie star devotees with access to cyberspace to pay tribute to the actor or actress of their choice by creating a Web page for them – i.e. a site of information, facts, trivia, pictures etc. on the World Wide Web – and the more popular the star, the more Web pages they will have in their honour.

While many of these are given over merely to biographical information and assorted movie pictures, it seems that Leonardo has captured the imagination of others in ways which other stars seem unable to inspire. One site, for example, is not so much a tribute to Leonardo but an on-line magazine which invites its readers to submit poetry and prose inspired by their Leo love. And all of them are beautifully designed and lovingly thought out – after all, nobody knows just when Leonardo himself might be sneaking a peek at them. 'I go on-line sometimes,' he admits. 'I like to go on just to see what people are saying about me. I get a kick out of that.' Some of his more recent interviews are only available on-line, a handful of which, when used by computer boffins who have very sophisticated equipment, actually offer the chance to hear him speaking. Despite the lack of shortage when it comes to web sites, two in particular stand out. The first of these is The Completely Unofficial Leonardo DiCaprio page (http://www.dicaprio.com) which claims to be 'the definitive source of information about Leonardo DiCaprio on the Web' and certainly doesn't disappoint. However, if it's links to further Leonardo info on the Internet you're after, then Fortune's Fool (http: www: teleport.com/~room101/calyx/leo.htm) is an absolute must to visit. It has its own Leonardo biography and facts, of course, but this site is a winner due to the brevity of its links to other Leonardo sources on the Web – including in-depth magazine interviews. In the end, it proves to be a positive oasis of information.

It does, indeed, appear that Leonardo mania is well and truly here to stay, while the man himself is fast living up to all those 'best actor of his generation' accolades. Whether he becomes the most bankable star in the world, or he continues to combine the big blockbusters with the small interesting offers that are thrown his way will be fascinating to watch, but with his amazing skills and his down-to-earth attitude, it looks as though things can only keep on getting better . . .

Leonardo guests at the premiere party for *American Buffalo* at LA eaterie Chasens

8 The Movies

Critters III

(1991)

(Guild Home Video)

Low-budget horror franchise which spawned a series of follow-ups thanks to its marginally successful 1984 original. Leonardo stars as one of the many folk bothered by an invasion of alien furballs (with very sharp teeth) in smalltown America. Almost identical to the two films in the series which preceded it, only fans desperate to catch a glimpse of everything in the Leonardo catalogue will find this worth viewing. **

Poison Ivy

(1992)

(Guild Home Video)

Leonardo co-stars with Drew Barrymore and Roseanne's Sara Gilbert, the latter as a high school loner who gets more than she bargained for when her beautiful, smart new best friend (Barrymore) turns out to be something of a Lolita. Dad gets seduced, mum gets picked off on the nearest balcony, and all manner of havoc is wreaked before the inevitable showdown makes its appearance. A little-seen but chilling tale, with the added bonus of Leonardo on teen buddy duties. ***

This Boy's Life

(1993)

(Warner Home Video)

Lacklustre box office aside, this powerful coming-of-age drama provided a showcase for Leonardo's considerable acting talents. Set in the 1950's, Leonardo stars as Tobias Wolff, a troubled teen having to cope with both the traumas of adolescence and the constant bullying from his abusive new stepdad (De Niro). Although initially this sounds like depressing stuff, it is ultimately an uplifting, hopeful story, with Leonardo's superb performance an indication of even greater things to come. ****

With Robert De Niro as a bullying onscreen stepfather, *This Boy's Life's* Toby is understandably worried

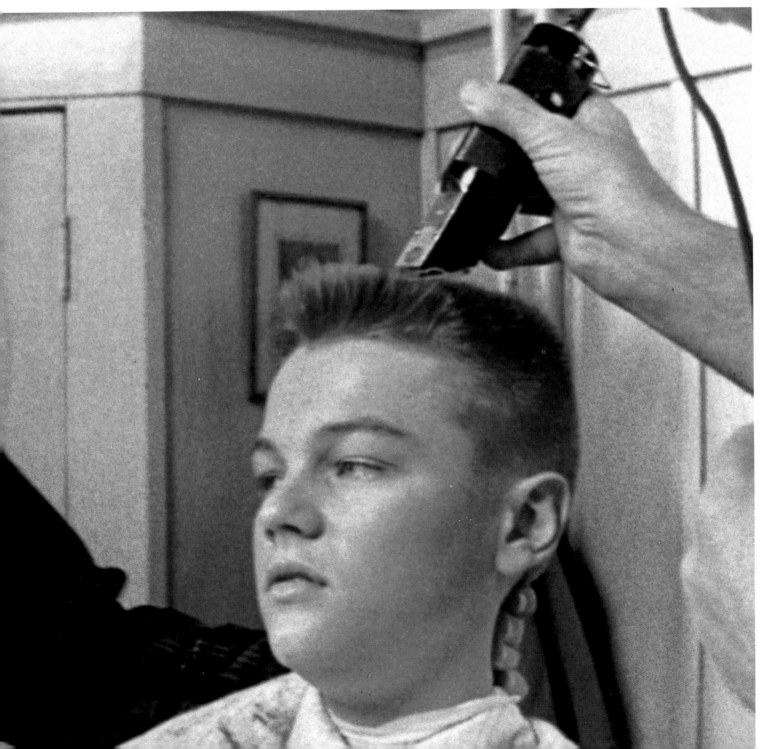

What's Eating Gilbert Grape?
(1993)

(Entertainment In Video)

The one which earned Leonardo a Best Supporting Actor Oscar nomination, something of a popular choice judging by the cheers when his name was read out on the night, and one which was thoroughly deserved. Based on the best-seller by Peter Hedges, this puts Leonardo on camera with fellow heart-throb Johnny Depp, in the hilarious, tragic and touching tale of Gilbert, a small town twenty-something who appears to be the only normal link in an outstandingly dysfunctional family; Mom (Darlene Cates) is a forty stone wreck incapable of budging from the sofa; sisters Amy and Ellen are downtrodden and brattish respectively, and then there's Arnie (DiCaprio), the mentally handicapped brother who has defied all doctors' expectations and is about to turn 18. Leonardo is nothing short of superb as the maddening but loveable brother, his vulnerability showing through to such an extent that many of his playful antics border on the heartbreaking. Juliette Lewis co-stars as the new girl in Gilbert's life, in a genuinely unmissable treat. *****

The Quick And The Dead
(1995)

(Columbia TriStar Home Video)

The closest Leonardo has ever come to starring in a commercial movie is this Sharon Stone-topped Western, an offbeat, exceptionally silly but deliriously entertaining slice of hokum. Known simply as The Kid, Leonardo is a brash gunslinger in a one-horse town, to which a vengeful female gunfighter (Stone), The Woman, has come for a spot of payback, and proceeds to shoot her way through a series of high noon duels before the real reason for her intended revenge, in the shape of local law enforcement Gene Hackman, is revealed. The ensuing action is tongue-in-cheek in the extreme, full of daft dialogue, Daffy Duck style comic book violence (the sun shining through holes shot through people's heads), and a glorious inability to take itself too seriously. And while this is only a supporting part for Leonardo, it's a fun one, as he gets to mess around with an array of Wild West

What's Eating Gilbert Grape?; a moment of
confrontation for Leonardo and Johnny Depp

weaponry and generally swagger around like a cool cowboy; in the end it's his comedic touch which wins the audience's sympathies the most. ****

The Basketball Diaries

(1995)
(1st Independent Home Video)
The thorny subject of heroin addiction gets an airing in this bleak picture, starring Leonardo as real-life teenage poet Jim Carroll, whose way with words and fondness for a spot of hoop-shooting was hindered by his tendency towards hard drugs.

The film chronicles his downward spiral from experimenting with illegal substances purely out of teenage curiosity (when we first meet him he is a promising high school student with an assured place in the basketball team), to his tragic drug dependency and relationship with his single mother (Lorraine Bracco), who decides the only way to get him off drugs is the hard way. Leonardo is compelling, backed up by an admirable performance from ex pop star Mark Wahlberg as his similarly drugged up best friend, and it's this which makes it impossible to tear your eyes from the

The Basketball Diaries **UK poster as it appeared in cinemas**

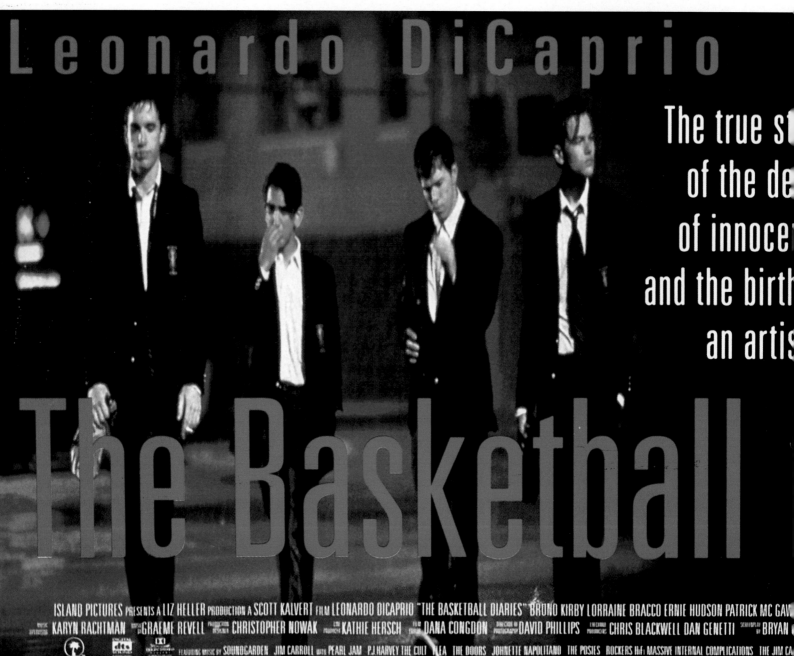

screen. Unfortunately Leonardo is much better than the film, which takes itself very, very seriously indeed; it is remarkably similar in storyline to the British smash *Trainspotting,* but like that film, the occasional dose of light relief would have made this far less of an ordeal. ***

Total Eclipse

(1995)

(not yet available on video)

Released in this country a good two years after it was made, this sees Leonardo in poetic mood yet again, starring as the 18th century French verse-scribbler Rimbaud, whose short, over-indulgent life came to a swift end in a gutter. British actor David Thewlis co-stars as Paul Verlaine, the older poet who became his mentor and eventually, his lover, and once they meet, it's downhill all the way, as they spectacularly live out the 18th Century equivalent of a sex, drugs and rock'n'roll lifestyle and it all turns sour. This is one of those films that really should be a superb, fascinating watch, but it goes for the arty approach instead, leaving a confused, strangely dull movie that lacks any clear sense of direction. And while Leonardo tries his best, it is soon obvious that his talents are better used elsewhere. *Total Eclipse* was originally all set to star John Malkovich and River Phoenix (Leonardo stepped into the breach after the latter's untimely death), and it somehow seems as though those two may have been better suited to the roles. Disappointing. **

William Shakespeare's Romeo And Juliet

(1996)

(not yet available on video – will be released by Fox Guild Home Video later in the year)

The film that finally proved both a critical and a commercial hit (guess who plays Romeo?) is the boldest, audacious version of a Shakespeare play to land on the big screen yet, and really confirmed Leonardo's status as both a heart-throb, and one of the best young actors of his generation. Australian director Baz Luhrmann (of *Strictly Ballroom* fame), takes the classic tale of two star-crossed lovers, brings it bang up to date, and leaves Leonardo and similarly acclaimed actress Claire Danes to utter the iambic pentamaters while looking longingly into each other's eyes and trying to forget the feud between their two families. The story does not deviate from the original, meaning of course that it all ends rather tragically, but there's so much to savour in-between; huge, monolithic towers, gun battles between the two warring families, the best party scene in ages, and Leonardo looking at his sumptuous best and acting his socks off; whether he's glimpsing Juliet through a giant fish tank, shimmying up the drainpipe to rendezvous with his new love,

MARK WAHLBERG ... JIM CARROLL
Z HELLER AND JOHN BARD MANULIS ...SCOTT KALVERT
E REVELL ... ISLAND ... PENGUIN BOOKS

Learning to fly: DiCaprio and Winslett on the prow of Titanic

James Cameron, the director of *Titanic*, holds aloft his Golden Globe for Best Film, surrounded by the main leads (l-r) Gloria Stuart, Kate Winslett, Leonardo DiCaprio and Billy Zane

he is an absolutely perfect Romeo. The Shakespearean dialogue, together with the story (love and marriage at first sight in this day and age?) may seem a little unconvincing in the setting, but suspension of disbelief aside, this is, from ear-splitting opening to the most heartbreaking *Romeo And Juliet* ending ever to see the inside of a cinema, absolutely superb. *****

Marvin's Room
(1996)
(Touchstone Home Video)
It may have been leading actress Diane Keaton who copped the Oscar nomination for this effort, but Leonardo still puts in some sterling work which was unfairly overlooked when awards time rolled around. Based on a hit stage play, Leonardo is the delinquent teenage son of Meryl Streep, a brash hairdresser who is forced to return to the family home she abandoned twenty years previously when it transpires that her sister (Keaton) has leukaemia. It's not too surprising to see why Streep's character fled to the city; this smalltown home, with its collection of oddball pensioners and the titular Marvin (a bed-ridden stroke victim) is far from happy, but over the course of the film relationships are re-forged, quarrels are had in abundance, and lots of tears are shed before everybody gathers round for the inevitable group-hug ending. Leonardo performs admirably, despite looking just a little too angelic to play a delinquent, and adds some spice to this sombre but enjoyable ensemble piece. ***

Titanic
(1997)
(To be released on video in autumn 1998)
Terminator director James Cameron's mega-budget tale of romance aboard the doomed ship is Leonardo's long-awaited break into the mainstream. The film, which has cost an estimated $200 million, features an all-star cast, headed by DiCaprio and Kate Winslet as a pair of travellers who have a passionate fling on board the Titanic before the inevitable iceberg hones into view. Also featured is *Twister* star Bill Paxton as a present-day seadog who investigates the wreckage (cue footage shot inside the actual waterlogged vessel itself). It would be unfair to disclose DiCaprio and Winslett's fate, but hankies are a definite requirement when watching this film. The movie is set to become the biggest box office sensation of all-time (it is expected to gross over $1 billion at the box office worldwide alone) and is also sure to clear up at the Academy Awards (it has a record 14 nominations). With his role in this film, Leonardo's career has gone stellar. *****

Jack (DiCaprio) holds Rose (Kate Winslett) close as the ship begins to go down

79

FILMOGRAPHY

Critters III (1991)

Poison Ivy (1992)

This Boy's Life (1993)

What's Eating Gilbert Grape? (1993)

The Quick And The Dead (1995)

The Basketball Diaries (1995)

Total Eclipse (1995)

William Shakespeare's Romeo And Juliet (1996)

Marvin's Room (1996)

Titanic (1997)